An Adventure More Exquisite Than Eyes Can Hold

By Victoria Fox

Copyright Page

Victoria Fox
Nazareth, PA

Simply This Publishing
Kindle Direct Publishing

INTRODUCTION

Through all the pain, the obstacles, and uncertainties our life is throwing at us, with determination and constant self – empowerment you will be able to succeed at your dreams and get where it is you are supposed to be. The way life works is not an easy task, it's a masterpiece with millions of pieces that are required to be particularly positioned. Furthermore, without a place of security, hopefulness, love, passion, and kindness you are not meant to be there. These are key components to a joyous life. Find that spot and release all tension. This book is abstractly written for you, beautiful humans, to interpret in a way your heart is longing for.

DEDICATION

  I would like to dedicate my writings and poems to my beloved older sister Angelica E. Fox. Through the years of maturing and developing, pain and sorrow, happiness and great successes, and love and encouragement, my deceased sister, Angelica, had put my mind in perspective at such a young age. Back in the year of 2009 my life was drastically altered; the loss of my best friend. I wanted to dedicate this book to a special person I hold very closely to my heart and that would be her. She's taught me, guided me, loved me, supported me, made me a stronger person growing up as a child, and mostly, was honest with me. I thank her, and think of her everyday.

Xoxo your little sister, Victoria

NOT ENOUGH

I just cannot get enough
Of a place so overwhelmed by life
Greenery and breath
Of cool waters and depth
Of sunny skies and lives
Of lullaby blues
Birds flying so high
Of summer felt days
The dancing leaves
Of greens so brand new
Walking barefoot
Connecting to life beneath calloused toes
The dirt claiming it's home
Laying on my clothes
On the ground that we so aggressively walk
Experiencing something so sweet
So mind soothing
Contemplating what to do next
What to bring on my way
My walk
My journey to my destiny

FEBRUARY 14-15, 2011

I really hate Valentine's Day
Broken
I like getting candy and presents, only
Singles awareness! Blah blah blah
It's all a big joke to me
Love is never as it seems
It's just puppy love
There isn't anything great about love... nothing
Someone says they love you...
What would you do?
What would you say?
Do they really mean it or don't they?
I don't know what to do
Help me
Please please please
I don't understand love at all
I don't understand life at all
It just doesn't make sense
Why are there problems in life?
Why do bad things happen to me?
I never have anything
Just why, why me?
It hurts when huge tragedies always happen to me
One thing that hurts me the most is that my older sister
Angelica got killed in a car accident
1.5 years ago
It was absolutely devastating for my family and I

Hearts torn
It's just not true
A false reality
No. never. Please no. just stop now!
She's gone and never coming back home to me
My angel. My best friend. My big sister.
I hate my life so much
What should I do? What should I say? Where should I go?
I'm so confused
Someone come help me
Tell me what to do with my life
I'm lost. I'm forgotten. I'm broken.
My life has fallen apart.
My heart has been ripped out of my chest
So much aching
So much sorrow
So much unbearable pain
I miss you Angelica
I will never let go of hope
Of knowing you might return to me
But I know it's not possible
I miss you dearly sissy
Please come back to me
I can't live
I can't breathe.

FEBRUARY 18, 2011

When you're feeling down
Have no where to go
You feel lost in this horrible world
It's terrible when you're alone
Lost. Alone. Gone. Black.
God help me please
Please
No one is nice to you
All they have to say to you is mean things
To put you down
They make fun of you
And leave you in the dust, alone
What to say
What to do
Where to go
This world is taking my breath
Just stupid
With no one to hold me
To love me
To adore me
Nothing
I'm broken on the inside
Just broken
Alone missing the one I loved most
A heart ripped to one million pieces.

LIFE

Keep a smile on your face
Each day you arise
Never take life for granted
The people who are placed
A path is decided
Along the way
Which a choice is given
You decide
A life of joy and happiness
Or a day with sadness resides
Be thankful and so dear
Life is a gift
And should be lived not by fear
Enjoy the good and even the bad
Be grateful and gracious
For the day is true

ANGELICA'S GONE

Angelica's gone
These days are passing
I don't know how come it came so fast
I never would've thought it would be her
She never hurt anyone
She was an angel to me
It shouldn't have happened to her
Death
Why couldn't it have happened to me
I will take her place
So she could stay
She couldn't displace her love
She made an impact on a lot of people
They never wanted her to go
Nor did mother and I
No no no she can't be gone
She's only been in this world 17 years
That is way way too young to die
I love her so much
That I think of her every second, everyday
I never do not think about her
Years fly down my face
And go to waste
And when I call her
She doesn't answer
Not even a "what?"
I look and scream
I cry out asking for her to come back

Just me alone with no sparing
Except with a broken heart piece
Bare inside
A million pieces lay
I'm extremely sad, with a little happiness inside
Fading everyday
With it getting harder and harder to handle
Just why my wonderful sister?
Why why why I ask
Oceans of tears filled with sadness
RIP sissy, I know you're gone forever
Your little sister, Victoria.

CROOKED LETTERS

 I write my worries on paper
For I know how I feel
My heart full of loss
With the keys lost
All I do is sit and stare at the sky
That's so high
With wonder in my eyes
With I see you fly
Will I see my sister again
Or will I lose trust in him?
She will be with me
It's been 12 of my own
I still don't know where she went
I'm looking and looking
Telling for you
I hope you're around my sissy
I want you near.

GROWTH

Keep growing
Alterations to the mind
Don't be blind
Keep growing
Alterations to the body
A temple of thee divine
Keep growing
Alterations to your spirit
Allow the internal awakening guide you
Reside in you
Keep growing
Alterations to the earth we embody
Become new, brand new.

DRIFTING PETALS

Flowers are so kind
So lovely and not so blind
The gentleness and softness
And purest of mind
They weep, yet they bloom
In the sun and by the moon
So lovely and not so blind
My dearest flower, my child
Thou art so kind.

AWAKENING

You awake so enthused, so poised
So calm, its dawn
A stroll in the city, so loud and so open
Sounds of the earth so unique and brand new
It has you thinking
"What can I do?"
Be true to yourself
So pure and so raw
Each thought in order and reaction on hold
On a shelf it sits
You think of a time
When life is so dull
Look. Listen. React. Reflect.
Those around you forget the thought told.

LOVE

All stress and anxiety fade away
When I look next to the body alay
I breathe so deeply
Share so completely
When I look in those bushes
The overwhelming anxieties, stressors, and fear fade away
My oxygen
My feet
My beat of life
So dear and so loving
So genuine and divine
You are mine
I say to you
I adore and love you.

UNIQUE

If you choose to be different
You choose a life of uncertainty
Absence of rules
Not caring
Not conforming
Not labeling
Not projecting
But ignoring and exploring

** Every Step Speaks Bliss **

POETRY

So authentic
So ambiguous
So raw
So relatable
But what lies within?
So much more debatable
Unpredictable.

WANDER

We will often wander
Where our life will guide us
Each step towards enlightenment
Is a guideline to our destination.

NIGHT GAZE

Nights filled with purity
Nothing but genuineness and laughter
A determined goal
What I live for, and more
What does life consist of?
So much negativity
Oh hostility
We become accustomed to bad habits
Thoughts and decisions
Surrounding yourself with a positive light
Held out by a guider, and provider
Allows you to lead yourself, and others
To reciprocate the act of kindness for which one has shown
Don't lose hope or ambition
Yes, a life's decision
Strive to live to its fullest
Exploring all that is offered
Each path, each road, and destination
Better than the last
Take a step forward
Take a step backward
You look at what you pose and absorb its importance
How blessed, so fortunate
Enjoying every aspect of life

The evils and the innocent
The successes and failures
And all other aspects too
Live without regret
Life through love.

MUST DO

Be a leader, not a follower
Be a light, not darkness
Be unique, not an imitator be
Be giving, not a thief
Be positive, not negative and
Be determined, but never lazy.

STILL

To decompress
Is to calm down
Which is to relax
To relax is to slacken
Which is to make less tense
Less rigid.

GOALS

Life is truly so sweet
So not clear, but apparent
Set goals
Have ambitions
Radiate positivity
Be relaxed
Calm. Cool. Collected.
Center yourself, become aligned.
Be kind to the world
And people around you
Say "hello," "good morning," "Avoir," "how are you?"
It's the smallest acts of kindness and consideration
That means absolute most
Make a difference
Be the change

SHINE

The reflection of the world
Lies within
Each stone
Each gem
Each shred of glass
Within the skies above

WISDOM

The earth is still
So stagnant and selfish
Greed fill of motionless smiles
If you listen closely
The screams of the helpless
Sing symphonies of hope
Louder than the ear can bare.

MESSY BRAIN

A messy brain
Is in comparison
To these trees
Each branch
Representing a thought
A thought that's formulated
Which, then, weighs your mind.

DEPTH

I fall deep
So deep
Within the depths of the earth's core
Within the roots of the forest
So dark
But yet so bright?
Such fright
So empty
But yet so fulfilled
So quiet
But yet so loud
Each rustle
Each crack
A new life is spun
A walk into the woods
Much deeper than expected
I'm lost
Yet I'm found
A sound which leads me
You find mystery
And stories
Within each peep
Silence.

TREE

Each stick
Each branch
Each petal
Each cacti
All working in unison
Creating the life it owns
All creating something
Something simply so powerful
So peaceful
So extraordinary.

WORLD

The world is abstract
So different than the next
So new
Each life is adjacent to the far
Yet somehow renewed
Each sound
Each touch
Each taste
And each feeling
So different from me as it is to you.

UNANSWERED MESSAGE

Your question what your next step may encounter
Whether it's a life changing moment
Or something as normal as a step forward
So arbitrary
Something so aesthetically good
Something so extravagant
Make it a lasting memory
A story teller moment
Reminisce
A day to remember
Smile and accept
Be happy
Look at those surrounding your person
The vibrations of cosmic energy
Their glistening personality
Shining so bright
Imagine their next move
The unknown
Alter that, if plausible
Make it your own
So known.

EXPLORE

Let's adventure
To the unspeakable
Even if there are roadblocks
Or detours along the way
Your perception will sway
Within each step
Taken along the way.

SOAR
EXPLORE
ADVENTURE
AND FLY
GET LOST
AND BE FREE.

SUNKISSED

Bring in the sunshine
So bright and blinding
A star as big as the moon
A celebration of life
Till death do us part
Keep a glistening smile
From side to side
Enjoying a life that is of one chance
To make it worth a million in one
You are required to have the feeling desired
Within yourself
Your heart
The sun as a stone
Of hope and eternal life.

PERK

Each sparkle
Each sprinkle
Each beam of light
Each smile
And laugh
Each bundle of joy
All creating
A memory of happiness.

REMINDER

Remind yourself that life itself is a privilege
Not a right
Very desired
We long for such invincibility
Yet we don't inhibit the ability
Without magical enhancements
We are just as little
As the ant walking
Building its colony
We are small creatures
Being a part of such indefinite time
A creation
Of variation
A memory
A conscious thought
It can be swiped
Vanished
Deteriorated
One blink of an awaken eye
We rise up to the open sky.

ENLIGHTENED WAKE

Ring, ding, dong
Wake up
Wake up bright and early
Take a deep breath
Inhale. Exhale. Release.
Get up and stretch
Stretch some more
Relax
Centered and aligned
Go for a stroll
Inhale a few more moments
Take in the fresh
Eat something fresh
No hurt or dirt
So delightful
Rejuvenated
Look around
Sky gazing
Listen to the world
The chirping of a birdsong
The swoosh of wallowing leaves
The pitter patter of tears we shed
A step
A glance
A moment of realization
Makes a moment of such importance
A though so divine
A memory that is mine.

SNOWFALL

The snowfall
So white and so elegant
Leaves no indent
But instead a sight
Of everlasting opportunity
And beauty
A glance so swift
So definite in motion
We find peace within
The winds
With a swish and a twirl
Of the cool breeze we inhale
So calming
So refreshing
We stand looking
With such a whirl.

CHANGE IN THOUGHT

A change
Change in thought
In heart
And in soul
Requires not much
But true intent
To do well
To be kind
To live
In our mind
In our heart
In our soul
A change in scenery
Permits in alteration
Alterations in attitude
In culture
In the state we reside
Struck with hopefulness
Beaming with unending love.

TORN

A heart so bare
So empty and destroyed
Lingers in the shadows
Of our own drowning terror
Those who we despise
Lays upon our feet
With so much anger
And hatred
So disingenuous
So unkind
We approach another without hesitation
Ill willed we be stilled
An act of self awareness
Must be at the forefront of each decision
No revision
Not for me, but for you
Think of now, not then
The past is unchangeable
The present is untamable
The future is imaginable
But that is what's most required.

APPRECIATION

We all are made up of something
Something we are given
Whether this be a luxury or a privilege
A kiss or bow
Given and appreciated
We give thanks
Each smile
And each stare
Filled with nothing but flare
We give thanks
To all within each lane
Not rude
Not ill willed
Not cold hearted
Not bare minded
We give thanks
To all within
It's a gift
From one we love
Which is a gift.

JOURNAL # 106

Family bondage will not be torn.
Friend bondage will not be stripped.
Listeners and seekers will be announced.
Liars and invaders will be destroyed.
But not from those who they are ruining, but from that of the world.
The power of those are ambivalent.
But the power of the truth is far from.
Choose to be ignorant or choose to be knowledgeable.
Make the decision quickly.
Our time is ticking.
The answers are dangling at arms reach.
Just seek.
Just listen.
Just believe.
Just choose to not allow others words become your current thought.
Current choice.
Be sure you have the power of your own. No judgment. No trap.
Allow all decisions be of which is felt to be true.
Just truth.

ROLE MODEL

We idolize
Conceptualize
Wearing a disguise
Upon our sheltered eyes
We comply with the lies
Our society supplies
And yet we always deny
All the signs
When time flies we cannot comply
Our daily life's lies
We must prioritize
Minimize
The debt we allow
Ourselves to apply
To our lives

We idolize
Conceptualize
As we live our lives
In disguise
Lying paralyzed
In design to signify
A life full of surprise
Within our lives
Becoming desensitized

Signs seem to be lies
But in the skies
My eyes on high
We choose to apply
But most likely deny

REALIZATION

Heightened thoughts
We are swallowed by the air we breathe
What's that mean to me?
I walk with hopefulness and insight
Such delight, I do not fight
I wonder what it is like to not be
So overwhelmed with curiosity
For the future
We grasp on the thinnest line of truth
Feels almost like a nooses
Don't allow our abridged brain be so loose
Those thoughts are not you
It feels like a flu
Which is empowered to consume you
Don't hit snooze on those who love you
Overcome that thought of what it is that is destroying you
A constant reminder of hope and light
Is if that you must fight
Disease, infection, infliction, addition
Those do not define you
But will refine you
You are a temple
Your mind, body and soul
Take control
You are capable, you are allowed, you can defeat
All demons and invaders
Said the eyes of the withholder

SICKENING

What's sick about this world?
Is people dehumanizing those around you
Because one loves another
Of an adjacent eye
Do not lie, no time
We live in a cruel world
So stick in the sand
Move right, not right
One step left, too straight
Heart crunching
Stomach punching
Mind stunting
Hand bunching
The hostility
Inhumanity
Drives us mad
Isn't it quite sad?

VIBES

  Everyone has a unique description of what this word means to them. I react heavily on what this universe tells me, how it makes me feel, how it incorporates its evil and its good, its arbitrary occurrences and their reasonings/purposes, and signs of design. All aligned as one; a circle of life. Been feeling a lot of energies of my surrounding people and my space lately. Cleansing and improving more often, and not allowing peoples' negative energies of life issues distract me from what is most important in life; that is to life it through love, honesty, and happiness. Vibing is when we connect on some deepened level of unconsciousness without there feeling a need to be unnatural or some other form of a person that is not your true self. We form this organic bond of purity and enlightened energies with humans, animals, and our earth which encourages us to let our person-our-temple be shown. When your intuition sets in, it allows you to depict what each person will do for you or if you will be able to. You feel it?

  How do you know when you're in positive space? What does the world provide you? What does your body feel?

  It's all about the connection we acquire when dealing with those who are dissimilar from us. Their personality, their physical appearance, their attitude and temperament, their desires and passions, their successes and failures, their hobbies and fantasies, their background and lifestyle, their daily routine and preferences, their behavior and perception on situations...

  We expect to form this eccentric connect through the works of our personal preferences being the leading factor in our decisions. We assume-which shouldn't be done- that our instinct will be accurate. We fail. No need to fret, we have the ability to recollect our thoughts and act on logical intuition next.

  Vibes? Those, which we state, are mutual feeling of acceptance, appreciation, genuinely appealing, and overall a good ass feeling with one or multiple people within the anew atmosphere. Furthermore, it is stated to be, "a person's emotional state or the atmosphere of a place as communicated to and felt by others-sensed intuitively." I stand by this. We all want to have a "good feeling" while in the presence of another. Whether it be a friend, family member, significant other, a boss, a co-worker, an employee, an acquaintance, but most of all a stranger. We long for acceptance and comfortability. Why? It makes life more thrilling and advantageous. Personal interpretation of one is a key objective in one's life. We want that feeling of goodness and peacefulness; longing for happiness and kindness. "Vibing" as we like to call it is a term used for years. It's precise and contemporary. I, you, we, us, he, she, they, all, want like things. We want to be vibe with all those around us living in an atmosphere and universal of opportunity and longing.

I want ONLY good vibes, POSITIVE vibes, and GENUINE vibes.

GRATEFUL

Always be grateful for what's in your life. Family -afar or near-, housing, food, clothing on your back, the love and support given, friends, your successes and failures, self-growth and self-worth, your body and health, your intellect and the fact that you take another breath day after day. - Never take anything or anyone for granted. Keep your eyes on the prize, and that is simply enjoying all that life has to offer you at each given moment. - Never take a moment for granted. Be grateful. Be kind. Give back, Always

Love one another; even those who hurt you. Unconditional love- even if it's from afar- gives those in need an ounce of hope and encouragement to keep moving on. So, never give up. Keep fighting. Keep giving. Keep living.

Explore, Adventure, Explore.
Your journey never ends.
Grateful

We will all reach our breaking point and feel so overwhelmed with life, but don't let that put your mind in a state of frustration and negativity! Let it be another lesson taught and learned from. Let it be a way to be mindful and connect to your inner self. Our books have multiple chapters still to be written. Your story is not over;

Keep pushing. Keep smiling. Keep surrounding yourself with rays of sunshine and green leaves; you ask the universe for answers, but ultimately you decide each step taken when moving forward.

DARKNESS IN MY VEINS

At some points in my life I feel absolutely nothing but pain. I feel nothing but loneliness. I feel nothing but being unwanted...unappreciated...thrown away...insecure...belittled...worthless...ugly...a waste of people's time...shamed...completely invisible. I feel majority of the time my cries are unheard and unnoticed. I feel I am never gonna make it. I feel as if an infinite state of a blank mind would resolve all unwarranted feelings which would make living a life of constant pain feel so much easier. I feel it would relieve me of such heaviness and shame. I feel life is way to unsustainable at times and I struggle making it day by day. I struggled, and still struggle.

It lasts for days...weeks...months...even years; A struggle of depression, anxiety, mental instability, wreckage, physical appearance, addiction and abuse. However, I feel as if no one cares or takes the time to try to understand me or even asks a simply question of:

"Are you okay?"

Or

"How are you doing?"

A feeling of my efforts and love not being reciprocated since my high school days. Those 4 years of my life were hell; nothing more. I have had everything taken from me.

This ranging from internal/personal, to family, to friends, to school in general; High school pushed me further and further out from society. It turned me into my own demon. This still carries into modern day. I say. I'm not here to gain pity. I'm not writing this to make you think I'm gonna take my own life or try to harm myself. Those days are passed me. Those were the old thoughts of mine that led me to a very dark stage in my life. However, all these feeling become so overwhelming and unbearable today that I have relapses. It makes me sick. It makes me come to a state of mind that ruins me all over again. It tears me apart for days...weeks...months...even years. I struggled, and still struggle...a lot. No one may know because it's not imperative for them to know and I don't want it to be known. Sometimes I just wish I genuinely had people there for me and actually care or me. I wish I could have people who were like me. Life is bad at times. We all just want that feeling of importance, comfort, wanting, and friendship.

I have hope I will become stronger each day.
I have hope life becomes better and better.
I have hope I can overcome absolutely anything.
I have hope.

REALITY

We become entirely blinded by a false reality
So tied into unrealistic expectations
So overwhelmed with societal obligation
That we become lost
Detached and ambivalent
Almost as if a single step in the correct direction
Is leading us into self destruction
However life is by far more than of our comprehension
It is an umbrella of opportunity
Of decision
Of desire
Of success
Of hopefulness
Of love
Each person is of itself
We, our own flesh and blood
Bone and nerve
Allow our mind to overcompensate
Our bodies, behavior, and attitude
We have the will power to become
A kind or queen of our precious temple
Keep your multiple eyes wide open
Look upon what is far and near
At last, one day, it will all become so very clear

1:11 AM

If you ever feel lost in a time of stagnation,
Know you will be found and life will become
Dependent on the movement of a foot.

NYC

One day I'll have a old fashioned VW van
One day I'll live in NYC; my final destination
One day I'll be traveling the entire world
One day I'll be completely free at mind
One day the world will be peaceful
Full of love
Full of possibility
Full of opportunity
And in favor of acceptance and equal rights
One day this world will be normal
One day
One day
One day

DAILY GOAL

My daily goal is to make another smile, laugh, chuckle a little, or a change in mood. I love to spread positivity, kindness, genuine vibes, and good thought. Why? Well, being happy with oneself can lead others to follow and to adopt your way of living each day.

Life is very, very short so why not live each day as if it's your last? Cliché I know. But it is the truest and most accurate phrase one can go by. It really pushes one to alter their view on life.

Enjoy your day even if it's pouring. Smile at a stranger, it can make their day 10X better. Hold a door open for a friend. Pick up garbage that lies on a table or the floor; keep our earth mighty and clean. Listen to music and get lost in the depth of the lyrics. Look at the sky and image the impossible, but make that thought come to be possible.

Just keep appreciating the earth and its natural beauty it withholds. Your life is important. Your person is loved. Your mind is powerful. Your body is your temple. Keep yourself well kept and allow your mind and body to work as one. Keep the good vibes coming.

MINDFULNESS

We take a step
A little deeper
A little closer
A little smarter we act
So smooth
So exact
The heart of the earth
So willing to react
One thought so wild
So unclear and unkempt
Absorbs the air
So sharp and mild
A moment of realization
That the world is of synchronization
We lose ourselves to the negatives
Of those who place themselves
In our path
We get caught up in a false reality
And lose a sense of personality
Your mind, body, and spirit so unclear
Leaves you with a tear
Regret and sorrow
But a chance that we want to borrow
Is taken away
But remember
Life itself is a gift
 Do not quit
Keep pushing forward

No room for hesitation
Be the shining star
And have dedication
Be a change in your own life. Be the reason you wake up in the morning. Allow yourself to realize you always have things you will have to work on;
Growing and maturing as a person. These are normal parts of life and becoming the person you want to become. Don't hold back, but move forward.
Life is tough
Don't ever think it's not
You have the power
Of your mind and body
Allow them to be united
Therefore, it will allow you to overcome
And conquer it all -
#MindAndBodyUnify

BE YOU

Don't ever feel awkward
Or fear rejection
We want to reach out
To those of objection
We want to create
A bond that lasts forever
With those of favor
You live life once
And can only enjoy it now
So take risks
Explore the world
Create new friendships
That you may have for a lifetime
Experience new places
New cultures too
Time is ticking
Days are twinkling
So find yourself
Be yourself
Without permission
From those surrounding you

GIRL PWR

It's so amazing to see other girls lift each other up rather than constantly tear them down due to jealousy, hatefulness, and inner insecurities being projected onto others to please oneself. The world is simply cruel, and we choose to be cruel. Stop the negativity and begin spreading positivity....always.

Be your beautiful, peculiar, and individual self w/o fear of being rejected, pushed away, or looked over.

MAJESTIC

Sunny day
A day so majestic
Full of sunshine and smooth winds
The rustling of leaves
The slight swish of the water blues
Remind us how not to abuse
A life we choose
So light and so white
We start to loose the light
Look around and see
The earth wants to please
The eye
The hand
The ear
The tongue
The rustling of the leaves
The slight swish of the water blues
Remind us how not to abuse
The life we choose

5 AM

5AM thoughts
So untamed and unfiltered
Overpower
And overwhelm
The mind we posses
We shelter ourselves
Our thoughts and obsessions
Let them free
For we want to see
Look through each lens
The primary two
And the third eye so true
Don't let the world around you
Cloud your view
For you are a creature
Of a world renewed.

OWNERSHIP

Just do your own thing
No matter the amount
Of negativity
Or hatefulness
Or disingenuousness
Or lies presented
Be you
Stay true
And you will
Overcome it all;

QUESTION

We wonder what a world would be like
Without creativity and individuality?
So mundane.
So ordinary.
No excitement.
Nothing to look forward too.
Tap into your inner self
And make something so fulfilling.
So you.

FRESH AIR

Wake up
Wake up bright and early
Take a deep breath
Get up and stretch
Stretch some more
Relax
Go for a stroll
Take a deep breath
Eat something fresh
So pure and delightful
So new and so raw
Look around
Listen to the world
The chirping
The swoosh
The pitter patter
Each step
Each glance
Each moment
All makes
All makes a thought
A moment so memorable

LITTLE THINGS

Enjoy the smallest things that life has to offer. Thus
including, the good and the bad. The failures and the
accomplishments. These things allow us to grow and
mature mentally and emotionally. We are so blinded by
what we all consider to be ideal, that we fail to realize and
accept what truly is real.
The earth so mysterious
So complex
And peaceful
Allows us people
To enjoy its features
It's significance
And it's meaning
The earth is continuously surprising me
My eyes are opened
To so much more
More than i could hope
And wish for
I thank you earth
For allowing me to soar
To a place of happiness
I crave so much more
Those experiences
I wish to share

RAINBOW RELATIONSHIP

A relationship is much like a rainbow.
A rainbow is a symbol of life, brightness, joy, and hopefulness.
A rainbow symbolizing excitement and passion, delight and admiration.
A relationship is all about love, commitment, loyalty, and forever.
A relationship symbolizing excitement and passion, delight and admiration.
Each color having its own significant correlation to a relationship and rainbow.

The RED is symbolizing such passion, loyalty and a strong love we share due to being so committed to one another physically, mentally, and emotionally.

The ORANGE is symbolizing success and courage. The success of being together for 3 years, 36 months, 1095 days, 156.429 weeks, 26280 hours, 1576800 minutes, and 94608000 seconds. And time is in counting.

The courage to let your guard down and be so vulnerable with me.

The YELLOW is symbolizing happiness, playfulness, and optimism. This color is the perfect one to describe our relationship. There isn't one day I go without smiling or feeling so overwhelmed with love from you.

The GREEN is symbolizing growth and encouragement. Each day each one of us help the other develop and grow as an independent individual. Each day we provide encouraging words to lift one another's self-esteem. I thank you the most for doing that for me.

The BLUE is symbolizing trustworthiness, tranquility, and communication. As I write this, these 3 are in the top five necessities in a relationship. These are crucial. I can say I trust you more than one may think.

The PURPLE is symbolizing spirit and harmony. Having a spiritual connection with each other, a type of connection of full understanding and agreement.

The PINK is symbolizing sensitivity, tenderness and gentleness. In our relationship, with such compassion and warmth from you, it makes me feel there is no end.

The BROWN, BLACK, & GREY is symbolizing mystery, sadness, disappointment, and troubles. With a combination of these four what will your relationship look like? Feel like? End like? I can share that even though we have our terrible times, you never give up on me and our love, and you help me push forward.

The WHITE is symbolizing purity, commitment and the unknown

FUN

It's not about having fun
It's more about being dumb
A slump
Beating to their own drum
Thumbs numb
Needing Tums
To make the feeling
Of being slum
Disappear
So inebriated

YOUR CHOICE

Life is what you make of it
Adventure any chance given
We take each for granted
Earth for granted
Our home and sacred place
We are blessed
Yet so blind
To all that is in front of the eye
Don't deny
Start being aware
Of the world you live in
And what is provided
Give thanks
To higher ranks
Give thanks
To that up high

SIGHT

You see what you want to see
Hear what you wish to hear
Feel what you long to feel
Walking to where your foot is guided
Through a mindless blueprint
A desired destination
Of a spirit projecting its tender heart

SELF

Do your own thing
No matter the amount of controversy
Hatred and ignorance
Do your own thing
For it is what you are meant to be
They will come to see
The real self is in front of thee

SUNKISSED

A ray of sunshine
Always brightening up my day
So friendly
So poise
No time passes away
I adore you
And your positivity too
So kind
And so beautiful
A day of sunshine
Please do not dwindle
But let's rekindle
Don't die out
My shining light
Or i will miss you

WILTED FLOWER

Each petal represents
Represents something different from the last
The insecurities
The dreams
The wants
The defeats
The longing of adventure
The happiness of life
The trials
Life itself
Our journey and story
Butt most importantly, you

PEACE

P practicing generosity
E expressing truth and intent
A acting with kindness and love
C coexisting and alignment
E expressing excitement and joy

BAREFOOT

We cannot get to our destined path if we are not willing to make one, two, three, four and more detours on the beautiful walkway your barefoot touches -that path is what we call our journey of life.

BRAND NEW

New beginnings are presented
Each rise of each day
Remember each lift of flesh is a gift
A gift from the provider and provided
A sunrise is a beginning, not an ending
Ending of time, not a crime
Tick tock tick tock
Time is rapidly becoming more discrete
Yet, there is a variation of distinct meaning
Unrevealing
One step, two step, three steps and more
Each giving us purpose
In a stride the truth lies
Remember each moment is for you, your reason
Not treason of society
Provider and the provided
A spot upon this washed world
A purpose and prize
Unrealized to these eyes

EMPOWERED

Empowered by the earth's way of telling us what we needed to hear, what we needed to see, and what was needed to be felt. The intricate the work of thought and love...I'm allowing myself to accept all that is in my walk on this planet, for each moment thus is providing me with lessons to be learned and remembered, and to fully digest all decisions made and obstacles that are presented.

EARTH DAY

  HAPPY EARTH DAY to this incredible place we call our home. A place we have the ability to breathe and create a life. Earth is home to more than just us -humans- so we need to be so grateful for this home. God is a creator with such magical power. Mother Nature is a giver and provider. There is so much life just living around you and you get to experience as much as they do. I don't know but to me nature and animals are incredibly important. Be kind and loving to our home and our family around us. Take prosper steps in making a change and making our earth a cleaner and livelier place. If you destroy nature/our earth, you are destroying yourself and the future. It begins with us.

IT'S O.K.

It's OK to love yourself; it's required.
It's OK to spoil yourself; it's desired.
It's OK to enjoy your own company; relaxing.
It's OK to not be able to choose; perplexed, conflicting.
it's OK to be proud of yourself.
it's OK to think you're a good person.
it's OK to know people lost you.
it's OK for you to feel lonely.
it's OK for you to not forgive.
it's OK for others to wanna copy you.
it's OK to have a panic attack.
it's OK to feel sad.
It's OK y'all

FOUNDER

We must grow through dirt to allow for a solid foundation. We must have faith we will develop naturally and of what is required our bodies to be. We must, then, allow for progression and regression; challenges and victories. We will sprout and become unified with oneself and that of the earth around us.

RA MA

An awaken eye from the depths of nothingness and alarm
hits six double zero
Repeated once, twice, three times
Sheets lining the cells of a body, with
Great warmth I elongate my brittle limbs
Sensations of ease in muscles so worn, so tightly wound.
An arm so aligned and in tune with thee enlightened moon.
Aligned with the bodies adjacent movement towards the
light. It's as if the flesh was as light as a feather, light airy
feeling of peace. Thee eyes yawn with such enthusiasm. The
morning air ever so kind. A sign.
One dreadful grunt that initiates the first step into routine.
The sun is at its peak, so sneak a peek; no blinks. The sun
reaching for our connecting drive. Swish! A gust of warmth
upon the naked face. Involuntary a smile appears. Ahh a
morning light crowns the beating of three within a poised
state. Universe I thank you, we thank, he/she/we/they
thank you. You've done too much. "Hello" a soften toned
murmur speaks. A sign, a signal, a devotion, a note. An
abundance of gracious comfort and entertainment
generates throughout the flow of blood. So warm and calm.
The body of I.
 • Ra • Ma • Da • Sa Hamsa I thank you •

POLAROID

Polaroid's make a photo more authentic and a thought
deeper.
Family bondage will not be torn.
Friend bondage will not be stripped.
Listeners and seekers will be announced.
Liars and invaders will be destroyed.
But not from those who they are ruining, but from that of
the world.
The power of those are ambivalent.
But the power of the truth is far from.
Choose to be ignorant or choose to be knowledgeable.
Make the decision quickly.
Our time is ticking.
The answers are dangling at arms reach.
Just seek.
Just listen.
Just believe.
Just choose to not allow others words become your current
thought;
Current choice.
Be sure you have the power of your own.
No judgment.
No trap.
Allow all decisions be of which is felt to be true.
Just truth.

THINK

Don't let the crazy in your life overtake your moment.
Don't let the crazy interrupt the memory in the making.
Don't define yourself by the way you thought the memory
was supposed to be: What it was ideally.
Live each moment thoroughly.

JUST STOP

- • stop • -
Stop with that petty bull-oney.
Stop with hatred.
Stop with violence.
Stop with racial discrimination.
Stop with unnecessary death.
Stop with wastefulness.
Stop with ignorance.
Stop with assumptions.
Stop with self harm.
Stop with altering your personality to match others.
Stop with self doubt.
Stop with gossip.
Stop with the constant desire to be better than the next person.
Stop with thinking you're entitled to anything or anyone; you're not.
You have the willpower and mental capacity to succeed at all.

MIND FOOD

I look religiously unto thee for the answers that are to be..
I watch and I listen..
I send thanks to those who are willingly giving..
I keep a sheltered tongue..
I keep a silent eye..
I keep a open heart..
But most of all.. I just observe..

R.E.M.

I shall dream of peace
That thou hast brought to me,
Who should say,
That through the midst it appears ideal
With you around there lies
A world free from confusion.
With thy breath full
We often dwell on subjects too great
For the eagerness speaking

GIVE

~ Always give ~
I give
You take
I give
What's now at stake?
I give
You ignore
I give
So unsure
I give
You steal
I give
What will we, she, he, they, reveal?
I give
You pretend
I give
What will be at the end?
I give
And you live
I give
You destroy
I give
You use my life as if it's a toy
I give, i give, i give
And all you can do is abuse the power it withholds.
~society~

LEMONS

  I stumbled upon a lemon today, prior to walking outside, through my stream of thoughts, I was thinking "when life gives you lemons, squish/(squeeze) and make lemonade"; a cliché phrase, as we all know. One may think this is a "bad" moment, but i thought of it as a great moment. Although the lemon lost its juice, it didn't become unusable; it became an object for something new to be created. Also, I love the color yellow, so it made me smile involuntarily. Make good out of what someone may think is "bad".

BROKEN

Don't leave a broken heart stranded
In the cold without anything to hold
No hope, no understanding
Just regrets and heartaches
We wonder
Through the nights under
Nothing will be brilliant
Without some resilience
A waste and broken
Unfixable
A decayed token
A body of mush
That's unforeseen
No improvement or alteration
Just a raggedy old heart
A waste and broken

SELF

A dream of soaring
one swing a swish
a heart so open
for a constant wish
no pain nor irrational thought
chase, chasing, chased
the overcoming, yet overwhelming
thought with such depth
I am where I am meant
desired
very required
I know you and see you
conspired yet not wired
your ugly heart will be fired
all will see
such evil and ill will
damaged, damned, done
keep soaring
exploring
a dream of unending
only one has rosemary

HOBBY

I thoroughly enjoy waking up early in the morning and admiring how beautiful the skies are: intrinsically and physically. It is breathtaking and brings out an immediate smile on my face anytime I see the colors of the rainbow. Thank you Mother Nature for your thoughtfulness and love you provide our eyes with. You're a true provider. AM Pennsylvania skies will always hold a place in my heart. I walk. I drive. I glide. I fly.

BE A LIGHT

Today is a good day
Get up and start your day off right
Look outside and listen to the world speak
Open your mind to new people and opportunities
Say hello to a stranger or compliment them
Smile
Try to be happy
You're still alive breathing
Walking
Living
Try to be happy

MORNING AIR

I'm just listening.
Go outside and listen.
Appreciation for nature.
Feels good to be alive.

RAOK

FRIEND-ly reminder
You are loved by those around you
Each ounce of kindness
Small and BIG
Mean a great deal to people
To myself
Some acts of kindness goes unseen
Unappreciated
Unheard of
But that should never deter you
Discourage you from continuing the behavior
Random acts of kindness
Goes a long way

DESTINY

Home is where you are truly happy.
Home is where you feel alive.
Home is where you can be your raw and complete self.
Home is where you feel balanced.
Home is where your mind is at ease.
Home is where your story had begun.
The Journey Continues

SPROUTING

You're like a plant
Each day you grow
A little more
And more
Your body longs for nutrition
UV rays
Warmth
Love
Care
Much like us humans
We long for all
Greatly
We grow each day
We flourish
We expand our horizons
We become who we are meant to be
To live
To die
Keep in mind you are allowed to shine
Bring in the sunshine
So bright
And blinding
Have a celebration of life
Keep a smile on your face
Enjoy each day
Of having another chance
To make a change
Within yourself

Within your life
Keep a pure heart
A pure mind
A pure body

CONTEMPLATING LIFE

As I was resting my head I came to the realization that being internally, as well as externally, satisfied and accepting of all that is around you, if you, and for you, you become more in tune with yourself, your surroundings, your mind and emotional state.

We let ourselves fall custom to all of the humans inability to become a independent and open-minded human. Instead, we come in contact with a stranger per minute, per hour, per day, per week, per month, per year...simply in a lifetime...and have the instant reaction to walk away; for most.

We as a community, a society, feel it is not our job in this world to become more involved or interested into those who we assume are a mold of perfection. We shy away and become hypocritical. We become self-centered. We become arrogant to those surrounding us. We become too consumed with pleasing oneself then to extend a helping hand or a speak a kind word to a listening ear.

We are in a constant battle with oneself. Our minds, our heart, our soul, our body all trying to cooperate as if they were one united beating flesh, but our efforts fall short and we are deteriorating; day by day. We are kept from moving on. We are kept from becoming a human of power. We stop ourselves from recognizing that there is hope, love, peace, and kindness still lingering in the air we breathe.

We need to reach far more than now.

We need to accept.
We need too understand.
We need to appreciate.
We need to be the change.
We need to...

??
Who am I?
Where is my destination?
What is my future?
When will I be free?
Why do we each get another chance to live and breathe?
How have I become so lucky?

NYC DAZE

June 4th, 2018:

The city is a place I feel so comfortable. It has a sense of welcoming and home. The city had always drawn me in from the very first time I've stepped foot into the glitz and glamour of time square. It's all about the atmosphere, the people, to vibes imitated, and the scenery.

As I take one step forward on the grounds of individuality, free-spirited, no-judgment zone of what is called the "Big Apple" I fall accustomed to their ways; a city that does not sleep. Therefore, I have time to be mindful of what is in our realm and formulate realizations. I had time to write. Explore the atmosphere. Collect my thoughts.

This particular visit of 12+ hours to the beautiful city of NY was one for the books. Why? Simply because it was one of the best experiences of my life. There were so many people i met, formed friendships with, got to connect with-vibe with, and learn from. It was of all ages; as young as 20s and as old as 50s.

I forever will remember this day. I spent a full day with a friend I hold dear to my heart as well as the place. I had multiple people, on multiple occasions compliment my aura, my personality, my fashion sense, my speech. It was truly so humbling and overwhelming to be surrounded by people who genuinely wanted to talk to us while visiting

NY. It was so awesome to see so many beautiful people in one place. It was so mind blowing to be surrounded by so many people who seemed to be full of happiness and love.

Times like this is what i live for. I love to be happy. I live to be free. I live in the moment everyday, all day. I live for experiencing new places and things. Life is so short y'all, you have to be thankful for each moment you have spent with those you love and for those who walk into your path, whether it be expected or not.

New York City, the people who where there June 4th, 2018, and the auras, I thank you for always exceeding my expectations.

SUNFLOWER

Baby sunflower
So not sour
I admire
And desire
Your higher power
Which requires
Very little
To be inspired
By the way in which you conspire
An occupier
A multiplayer
One may call you a purifier
So bright and happy
I search for you
Document you
Become you
So sweet and so innocent
A flower so intricate
Makes me want to recreate
Each wind instrument

STUCK

We are stagnant.
We are oppressed.
We are mundane.
Don't allow these words to lead your life.
To predict your future.
To limit you from becoming who you are meant to be.
You have complete control
Of your mind, body, and spirit.
You are observant.
You are curious.
You are spontaneous.

INTENTIONS

True intent is very important. Acting upon what is true and appropriate gets you further than being someone you are not and basing your life on unrealistic expectations and intentions. I stand tall. I am who i am. I have who I have by my side because they want to be there and those who remain are forever appreciated and cared for. I am an open book. You see the real me.

Grateful: We will all reach our breaking point and feel so overwhelmed with life, but don't let that put your mind in a state of frustration and negativity! Let it be another lesson taught and learned from. Let it be a way to be mindful and connect to your inner self. Our books have multiple chapters still to be written. Your story is not over;

Keep pushing. Keep smiling. Keep surrounding yourself with rays of sunshine and green leaves. You ask the universe for answers, but ultimately you decide each step taken when moving forward.

SMILING

Today I woke up
So happy and energized
Full of laughter and smiles
Definitely recognized
I say good morning sun
And to the skies and birds
So synchronized
I got ready for my day
Wrote in my journal
A happy thought and dream
So very organized
I took a picture of the earth
And said what a beautiful day
With no disguise
I walk outdoors to a car
Drive to my friends who waits
Each tune aligned
To each road stop sign
I continue to laugh and smile too
A day of blessings
From me to you

BIRTHGIVER

Dear Mother,

I wake up smiling
Smiling because I know I have you by my side
Smiling because I know you love me
Smiling because of your positive persona
I wake up smiling
Feeling so full of thankfulness and happiness
Knowing I can come home to someone
Someone who will be there forever
I wake up smiling
Because of such a positive attitude
A positive personality
A positive perspective on life
I wake up smiling
Smiling from ear to ear
Because I'm overwhelmed with such security
With such honesty
With such selflessness
I wake up smiling
Where it brings tears to my eyes of such joy
And butterflies to my stomach of such
Such unconditional love
I thank god, daily, for you
Words will never describe how much
How much I adore and care for you
I wake up smiling
With so much to give to you

Through a smile
Through a hug
Through laughter
Through gifts
And simply
An I Love You
I wake up smiling

CLOSER TO THE CENTER

One step at a time
Moving closer to the sun
Each bean of sunshine upon our skin
Each strand of grass
Between each toe and finger
So delightful
So soothing
Nature is a blessing
And so insightful

CLOSER

Given so much more than ever expected.
So astonishing and liberating.
The sprinkle and splash.
The beam of sunshine on my skin.
The laughter of a lover in the distance.
A world of natural beauty.
Forever being blessed.
Thank you God
For your exceptional creations.
#everydayisearthdayforme

BLISS

Life as a whole can be described as two
This consists of the great days and the okay days. Today
was a combination of both
Yet I didn't let the unfortunate events limit me
From enjoying a sunshine filled day with exotic winds. You
have to take every moment
Encountered as a lesson
It was meant to be learned
All the people, places, and events
Make your day and life worth while
Be thankful everyday
For another breath taken
Spread an encouraging thought
And positivity each and every day
Be the light
That someone doesn't have in their life.

FRIEND

Dear friend,
A ray of sunshine
Always brightening up my day
So friendly
So funny
No time away
I adore you
And your positivity too
So kind
And so beautiful
A ray of sunshine
Please do not dwindle
Or ill will miss you

FORESHADOW

I've never come across
So many people in one day,
In such a short period of time,
Who seemed to be so unsatisfied, unhappy,
And unappreciative of life and people in it
It saddens me to see such unhappiness
As I walked past
I share a smile
This simple act of kindness goes a very long way.
Be the person you want to be
Spread positivity
Be a light in people's lives
You don't know how much of a difference it can/will make.

EXPLORE

Let's adventure to the unspeakable
Even if there are roadblocks
Or detours on the way
Your perception will sway
Along the way

NEXT MOVE?

You question what your next step may encounter
Whether it be something so arbitrary
Something so aesthetic
Something so extraordinary
Make it a memory
Make it a day to remember
Smile
Be happy
Look at those around you
And see their personality shine
Imagine the way they think
Imagine their next move
It's all the unknown
So alter that
Make it known

FALLEN APART

A messy brain
Is in comparison to these trees
Each branch represents
A thought
An idea
A goal
That's formulated
Weighing your mind
So heavy

DISSIMILAR

If you choose
Choose to be different
You choose a life
Of not caring
Not wondering
And ignoring
What people say
What people think

LAUGHTER

Laughter is the best medicine
Even if you feel so worn out
Or as if life feels so consumed with negativity, unkindness.
Just know, each day gets better
Gets brighter, and gets happier
You share, a sincere smile
You give a helping hand
But it means nothing to most
People are so focused on the negatives in their life
They've forgotten to appreciate what they do have
Always be kind
You NEVER know what your hello, how are you, smile, or
kind deed will do
In someone else's life
You could be the reason he and/or she takes another
breath.

FIRE

A fire so brilliant
So fierce and resilient
Puts fear in the mind
Creating us to become quiet
Still
Non responsive
Don't let the spark of uncertainty
Continue to fuel the fire
Let it explode
Until someone knows

1:11 AM

If you ever feel lost in a time of stagnation
Know you will be found
Your life will become dependent on the
movement of a foot
Not someone else's but yours
The power lying in your hands
Fate, eternity
Life beyond

PEACE OF MIND

We wonder if we will ever feel at ease; peace of mind. We wander to make it happen. We assume we will never be at a level of complete tranquility and soothing, however that is far from the truth.

We all have the power to do and feel as we please, as we hope for, as intended to do. You have to believe that you are strong enough, brave enough, and have the internal agility to create peace.

Becoming one with oneself is the key component to reaching this reachable and obtainable goal. Others find pleasure in always assuming and projecting their insecurities and envious state onto those who have their life in order, who are succeeding, or are presented with a countless amounts of opportunity. How is that fair? we ask ourselves.

Instead of surfing to a negative and aggressive behavior and thought we all have to try to find peace; tranquil thought. We tap into our bodies reaction of fight or flight sensors. That may not be the most clever choice of action however its instinct. We need to find balance in mind and body. We need to keep our bodies at a fixed state. We need to think ahead.

Life is about finding "peace of mind".

Search for peace.
Practice peace.
Project peace.
Live by peace.

YAWN

I thoroughly enjoy waking up
Early in the morning
Admiring how beautiful the skies are: intrinsically and
physically.
It is breathtaking
Brings out an immediate smile on my face
Anytime I see the colors of the rainbow.
Thank you Mother Nature
Thank you God
For your thoughtfulness
And love you provide our eyes with.
You're a true provider.
AM Pennsylvania skies
Will always hold a place in my heart.
I walk.
I drive.
I glide.
I fly

WALKING ON CLOUDS

Self realization
A heightened account of recollection
Breathing in
Breathing out
Imposing peacefulness
Upon the body of those who sit
A luxurious sight
Oh my dear eyes applauding
A gust of warmth
So overwhelmed with gratitude
Long gasp shared with you
Inner mind recognizing
Today is not just another day
It's one of rebirth
Another day of life, well lived
Another change required
Most desired
I walk upon the cushion of hope
Of serenity, and of up most love
An overall body formulation of great joy

HANDS

The hands extended with cosmetic energies
Grateful. Thankful. Blessed.

MISS YOU

Your beauty overwhelms me.
You're a symbol of a hello
I say hello to you my sister, Angelica
From above
Flying so high
I miss you
But I feel you

JUST STOP

Stop with that petty bullcrap.
Stop with hatred.
Stop with violence.
Stop with racial discrimination.
Stop with unnecessary death.
Stop with wastefulness.
Stop with ignorance.
Stop with assumptions.
Stop with self harm.
Stop with altering your personality to match others.
Stop with self doubt.
Stop with gossip.
Stop with the constant desire to be better than the next person.
Stop with thinking you're entitled to anything or anyone; you're not.
You have the willpower and mental capacity to succeed at all.
Stop. Think. Reconsider. Recognize. Alter. Reflection. Action.

MOMENTS

Don't let the crazy in your life overtake your moment.
Don't let the crazy interrupt the memory in the making.
Don't define yourself by the way you thought the memory
was supposed to be: what it was ideally.
Live each moment thoroughly.

STILLNESS

I sat in deep thought
Within the cold breeze
That layered my body.
A droplet or water fall
And crests my hand.
A tightly wound grin
That appeareth upon thy face.

YOGA

My goal: I can improve on a whole other level after dedication, consistency, recollection, mindfulness, peacefulness, and acceptance of what my body and mind are able to accomplish in unison.

Very new "things" take an unlimited amount of practice and effort. If you cannot practice these two key aspects of importance together you will not be able to reach your personal goals and acquire a new found appreciation for your mind, body, and spirit partnership.

I try my best. I work towards success. I put in effort and time. I simply believe and have hope I'll master each pose and soon be able to understand and master the more complex stretches and poses of yoga as well in the future.

AUTHOR PAGE

My name is Victoria Fox and I reside in Nazareth, Pennsylvania. I have been writing poetry and short writings since I was a young adolescent dating back to the year 2009. Writing sparked my interest due to an event, a tragedy nonetheless of my older sister Angelica Fox, she had gotten killed in a horrific car crash in '09; I was only 10 years old. For ways in which I could grasp this occurrence and cope with such a tragedy, was with paper and a pencil. It was such a peacemaker within my mind and heart, as well as the love of God. My faith truly guided me through it all! Not only was God an adequate influencer and provider, the earth and its amenities overwhelmed my person and cradled me through my journey of what is known as "life." Nature, my home, gives me pure contentment and serenity each and everyday. I would not be as I am today without the self-love, determination, positive mind set, and love of family and friends.

71282230R00073

Made in the USA
Middletown, DE
30 September 2019